HOW TO START *YOUR OWN* BUSINESS

By Alvin Granowsky
Illustrated by Liz Callen

MONDO

To my grandchildren, Aaron, Marc, Emma, Alexander, Nicholas, Elizabeth, and Elena with love and hope that they will be able to earn their own way through life

—A.G.

For information contact:

MONDO Publishing,
980 Avenue of the Americas,
New York, NY 10018

Visit our website at www.mondopub.com

Printed in USA

09 10 11   9 8 7 6 5 4 3 2

ISBN 1-59336-813-3

Designed by Witz End

Table of Contents

Have you ever thought about starting a business? There are many opportunities just waiting for the right person to come along. Some businesses make a **product**, such as lemonade, chocolate chip cookies, or greeting cards. Others sell a **service**—mowing lawns, pet sitting, or teaching people how to use their personal digital assistants (PDA's) or DVD players.

To start, take a look at this list of products. As you read, think about which ones interest you and which ones you'd be successful selling.

Products to Make

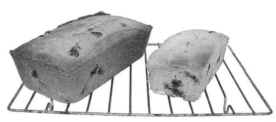

- Cool drinks (lemonade and iced tea)
- Baked goods (chocolate chip cookies, brownies, cinnamon rolls)
- Jewelry (bracelets, necklaces, and rings you've designed and made yourself)
- Books (for example, favorite recipes or riddles and jokes—written by you)
- Greeting cards (handmade by you)
- Stationery with customer's letterhead
- Seasonal decorations

These products are just a few of the things you could make yourself. As you walk around town, shop at the mall, or even watch TV, look for other items that you could create and sell. People think of **innovations** every day.

In addition, there are many other products that may be too hard or expensive to make yourself. You could act as a **distributor** for these products, which means that you would sell them for a **manufacturer**. You might consider selling magazine subscriptions, personal-care products such as soaps and shampoos, or candies. In fact, you may have already sold products such as these in school fund-raisers or for social organizations. However, you can also contact the manufacturers directly and go into business for yourself. A good place to start is with the website www.fundraising.com. There are products you can purchase at a **discount** and then sell for the regular price, keeping the **profit**. Check out www.dollars4kids.com for more ideas.

Another option is to sell a service—something you'd get paid to do that would give other people more free time. Here are some ideas:

Services to Sell

- Snow shoveling
- Tutoring
- Lawn mowing
- Grocery shopping
- Pet feeding
- Garden weeding
- Plant sitting
- Housecleaning
- Window washing
- Dog walking
- Giving computer lessons
- Entertaining at parties
- Delivering newspapers
- Golf caddying

These lists are far from complete. They're meant only to get you thinking about a business opportunity that might be right for you. There are so many business opportunities just waiting for the right person to come along. To get other ideas, flip through the business listings of your local telephone directory. You will be surprised by how many types of businesses there are.

From these listings write down the products and/or services that interest you. This is your first step to starting your own business. But it takes more than just an interest in something to be successful. The next step is to ask yourself, *What am I good at?* or *What could I be good at?*

 Tip → You'll find some very helpful ideas and suggestions for starting a business at www.teachingkidsbusiness.com and www.youngbiz.com.

Chapter 1

What Are Your Talents and Interests?

Once you've decided to start a business, the first big question to address is what type of business you'd like to start. To answer this question, think about your talents and interests. This doesn't mean you can't expand your interests or improve your skills along the way, because you can. You surely will learn new things and get better at what you already do well.

Choose a business that involves something you like to do. There's no point grinding away at something you don't really enjoy. The more you enjoy doing something, the more willing you will be to put in the necessary time to learn and get better at it. Being naturally good at something is important, too. You need to figure out both what your talents are and what you enjoy doing, which will help you find the right direction.

Let's say, for example, that you like baking and eating but dislike anything related to mechanics, like fixing your bike or learning how cars work. Which business idea would make the most sense for you—making and selling chocolate chip cookies or offering a repair service for broken bicycles? Don't just choose the first idea that seems like a good one—really think about it to decide what's best for you.

Make a list of your talents and interests, then match them with various business possibilities. For example, see the following chart:

Talents	Interests
1. Animals like me. 2. I am good at figuring out what animals need or want.	1. I love animals of all types. 2. I enjoy playing with pets or just watching them. 3. I want to learn everything I can about animals.

Business Opportunities for Right Now

- Dog walking
- Pet sitting
- Pet bathing and grooming
- Dog training

Future Business Opportunities

- Opening a pet care and grooming shop
- Becoming a veterinarian and opening my own animal hospital
- Running an animal training school
- Working at an animal preserve

By now you've made a list of business ideas that seem interesting. You have also thought about your abilities. Now you need to find the best business opportunity to go with your talents and interests.

Chapter 2

Searching for Opportunities

Starting a business isn't just about you and your interests and abilities, however. The customers you hope to serve must also be considered. They are the key to your success or failure as a businessperson. You have to figure out how to fill the needs and wants of the people you hope to serve. Let's consider some of the best ways to do this.

Start by Listening

People are always talking about their problems, needs, and desires. Have you ever heard people complain about not being able to work their new DVD player or fancy cellphone? They've purchased equipment with wonderful features but can't figure out how to use it! Well, their difficulties can lead to a business opportunity in electronic **consulting**, if you have skills and experience with electronics.

CAUTION!

Be sure you know what you are doing before you start working on someone's expensive product.

Tip → To learn more about the products you will be helping people with, check out the websites of the companies that make those products. Many offer on-line training and guidance on how the items work. You can also get training from appliance stores that sell the product.

Have you ever overheard friends or neighbors wondering who will care for their pets while they are on vacation? Those concerns can be a great business opportunity. Elderly people often need assistance walking, feeding, or even playing with their pets. You may be just the one to fill this need.

CAUTION!

Be sure you are aware of everything that's involved in caring for someone's pet (including the name of a vet, in case of emergency) before you agree to take on the responsibility.

Tip → Before agreeing to a job, meet the pet and, while in the presence of the owner, go through a trial run of what you will be required to do. Work out your responsibilities with the pet owner and write them down. Photocopy this **contract**, and each of you should sign both copies. That way, you will each have a signed contract stating what's expected.

Ask Questions

Sometimes it takes more than just keeping your ears open to discover what business opportunities are out there. Ask around! Doing so could help you uncover a new business opportunity that you hadn't thought about, or reveal a different way to approach the business you are considering. Asking questions could also confirm that you are on the right track. Or it could show you that your idea is faulty and that your business will probably not succeed. This could save you a lot of time, worry, and money.

Develop a **questionnaire** to survey the needs and wants in your community. You can contact friends and neighbors, and then branch out to others in your community. What questions should you ask in a questionnaire? If you are thinking about starting a pet-care service, you might create a questionnaire along these lines:

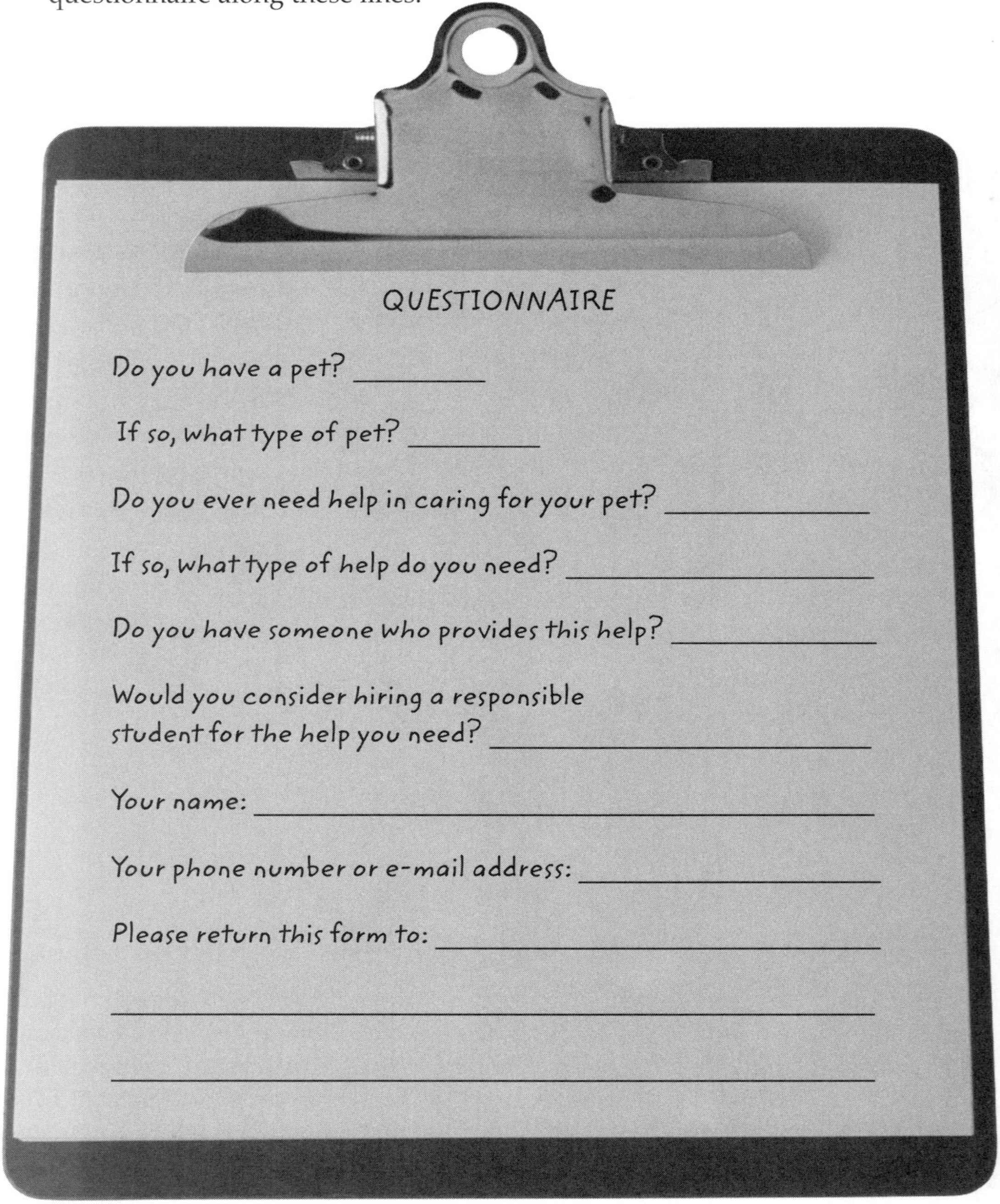

QUESTIONNAIRE

Do you have a pet? _____

If so, what type of pet? _____

Do you ever need help in caring for your pet? _____

If so, what type of help do you need? _____

Do you have someone who provides this help? _____

Would you consider hiring a responsible student for the help you need? _____

Your name: _____

Your phone number or e-mail address: _____

Please return this form to: _____

_____

_____

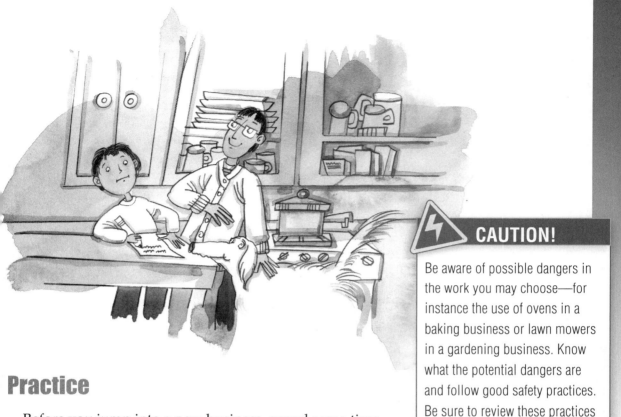

CAUTION!

Be aware of possible dangers in the work you may choose—for instance the use of ovens in a baking business or lawn mowers in a gardening business. Know what the potential dangers are and follow good safety practices. Be sure to review these practices with a parent or guardian and have them supervise you, when necessary.

Practice

Before you jump into a new business, spend some time working for someone who does that particular kind of work. There is no substitute for experience and no better way to get it than working for someone who knows the business. What you learn on that job can help make you successful in running your own business.

Pitfalls to Avoid

It would be a mistake to start a business without considering potential customers' needs and wants. No matter how hard you work, if you are providing a product or service that people are not willing to pay for, it is unlikely that you'll succeed.

For example, think about how difficult it would be to sell raincoats in the middle of a desert, where it hardly ever rains, or winter coats in the tropics, where it never gets cold. People won't need or want these products and won't buy them no matter how good they are or how much hard work is put into selling them.

Chapter 3

What Do You Want From Your Business?

Starting a business is a serious task. It will take a great deal of time, energy, planning, and possibly money, too—since there may be **start-up costs**. So before going any further, you need to think through what it is you are hoping to get out of your business. This will help you decide how much time, energy, thought, and money it is worth **investing**. At first you'll probably have to invest more than you get back. Set a limit of how much time and effort to devote to starting your business. Ask yourself the following questions:

Am I starting a business...

- to make money for a one-time need, such as a new computer or a trip with friends?
- to make money for ongoing needs and entertainment, such as clothes, movies, and snacks?
- to make money to help my family through a difficult time?
- to make money to help my family on an ongoing basis?
- to make money to put into a fund for college?
- to stay busy during summer vacation or other free time?
- for the learning experience and to prepare for the future?
- to challenge myself and find out if I can actually do it?

There can be more than one reason to start a business. Just make sure your goals are clear so that you know how much effort to invest. If a business is just something to keep from being bored during summer vacation, you might not want to spend as much time or energy to make it work. If the money you are hoping to earn will go toward helping your family through a rough time, it may be worth a great deal of effort. The more important the goal, the more time you should put into developing your business.

Also remember that goals can change over time. What may have started as a desire to earn money to buy something special could turn into a source of money for college, or even a potential lifetime career!

Chapter 4

Don't Bite Off More Than You Can Chew

Have you ever heard the expression "Don't bite off more than you can chew"? It makes a lot of sense. Don't take on more responsibility than you can handle. Be realistic about how much time, energy, and money you will actually be able to put into your business. The danger is becoming too excited about all the possible benefits you might get from your business, and then trying to do more than is physically possible to make sure that you don't fail. It's important to consider carefully how much time and energy you actually have to give.

Once you figure out how much time you spend at school and doing your homework, you'll probably find that you don't have much free time left for a business. You might have lots of free time over the summer, but what happens when school starts again? Will your business continue to be successful once fall comes around? Don't forget your extracurricular activities, like sports, clubs, or playing a musical instrument. In addition, you probably have family responsibilities, such as daily chores, that will take up some of your free time.

Remember that your business is just one part of your life. As exciting and rewarding as it may be, you should be careful not to let it get in the way of your responsibilities. Set aside some time each week for relaxing, playing with friends, and other fun activities. A balanced and well-rounded life is important to staying both healthy and happy.

How much time do you really have to devote to your business? How many hours do you have on ordinary school days? How about on weekends and vacation days? Once you have figured out what your responsibilities are and how long they will take, then you will be able to make realistic decisions about what you can or cannot commit to. For example, during the summer you might be able to spend five days a week, eight hours a day on a gardening service, but once school begins, you will have to cut back. Once you've figured out how many hours you can spend on your business, think about whether it's sufficient to get your business up and running. Will your business be able to succeed with this amount of time and effort?

Don't make any promises to customers that you won't be able to keep. For example, if a customer is depending on you to mow his or her lawn on Monday morning and you need to be at school at that time, that's a big problem. If you want to be a successful businessperson, you must anticipate these sorts of conflicts.

Think about what you can and cannot do, and make sure you live up to your commitments to customers. Remember, you want to hold on to their business: you do not want them spreading the word to potential customers that they can't trust you. If you are honest about what you can and cannot do, most people will appreciate your honesty. The best way to make sure that you and your customers understand each other is to talk freely and work out problems quickly.

 CAUTION!

Tools like hedge clippers and lawn mowers can be extremely dangerous. Be sure you have permission from your parent or guardian if you plan to use one.

Chapter 5

To Make Money, You Have to Spend Money

Another important question to consider when starting a business is what it will cost to run. There are start-up costs and **ongoing costs**. Start-up costs can be high for lawn-mowing, hedge-clipping, and garden-weeding services, for example. Your customers may expect you to have your own tools, which means a lawn mower, edger, hedge clippers, and fuel. Where will you get these items? If you have to buy them, where will you get the money?

Getting the money necessary to start a business may be difficult. An adult who wants to start a business can go to a bank to present a **business plan** and apply for a **loan**. The bank then evaluates the business plan, the applicant's experience, and his or her **credit rating** to determine whether the person is likely to have a successful business and will be able to pay back the loan and **interest** charges. If the **loan officer** thinks the business has a good chance to succeed, the bank will approve the loan.

Tip → Many adults are happy to teach young people about starting and operating a business. A loan officer at your local bank may be willing to review your business plan with you and make suggestions to help your business succeed.

However, banks generally don't give loans to kids. So your best bet may be to discuss your business plan with a parent or another older, experienced relative or friend. Together you can figure out how much money will be necessary to start your business. You will need to list your precise start-up costs. Instead of guessing, do your homework. List all of the equipment you'll need, and find the actual cost of each item.

Think about where the money might come from. Do you have some money in a bank account that can be used for this purpose? Are your parents willing and able to lend you needed funds? Perhaps you can work briefly for someone else to save up the needed money. List your options.

In addition to start-up costs, there are ongoing costs. For example, say your business idea is to create and sell a product such as greeting cards or chocolate chip cookies. The ongoing costs would include the materials that go into producing the product, whether it's paper and art supplies or ingredients such as flour, sugar, and chocolate. The point is, it costs money to start and run a business. Be aware of these costs and think about how you'll pay for them.

Tip Instead of buying everything you need to start your business, consider renting or borrowing. You may be surprised to find that you know someone who is willing to lend or rent equipment to you until you've made enough money to purchase what you need. Discussing your plans and needs with others may prove helpful in finding sources you hadn't thought about. Word gets around, and people are often willing to help.

Pitfalls to Avoid

You may not have the money to start and run a business, and you may have trouble getting money. But don't let this make you give up before you even start! To be successful in any task, you must think positively and be patient. View each problem as a new challenge. By paying attention to the problem and thinking about different ways to solve it, you will usually come up with a great solution. You don't have to do it alone—ask friends and family to suggest some ideas. Even if you are sure you've thought of every possible solution, other people will often see things in a different way and come up with other approaches.

Chapter 6

How Much Should You Charge?

Setting the right price for your service or product is important for your success. If your price is too low, you may get a lot of business but you may not earn enough to pay for your costs, time, and energy. On the other hand, if your price is too high, you'll attract fewer customers.

Here are some rules to follow when setting a price:

- Your selling price has to pay for your costs with enough profit to make your efforts worthwhile.

- Your selling price has to be in line with what your **competitors** are charging. Make sure you're not charging too much. After all, why would customers pay you $8 for a geranium plant if they could purchase a similar one for $5 elsewhere? Don't charge too little either. Then you'll be taking away from potential profits. Ask your family and friends what they think would be a fair price.

- Keep in mind that you will be able to charge more if you offer extra features or better quality than your competitors. You will need to point out and explain these "extras" in your **advertisements** so that customers understand why your price is higher. For example, if you **guarantee** that the plants you sell will live for one year after purchase or you will replace them for free, and your competitors do not, then you are providing a benefit that customers might pay extra for. Or if it's a service you are providing, such as mowing lawns, make it clear that you do edging work and remove the cut grass for no extra charge. If this is something your competitors don't offer, customers will hire you for the additional value.

Be very clear when you tell the customer about the added benefits your product or service provides.

- You need to understand the difference between what your potential customers *expect* to pay and what they are *willing to pay* for your service or product. It's an important difference. The price you set may be what people expect to pay for that particular service or product, but that doesn't mean they actually will buy it. An example of this can be seen in the high-end bicycle market. People may expect a top-of-the-line racing bike to cost over $2,000, but most people just don't have that kind of money to spend on a bicycle. So it doesn't really matter that they know what to expect to pay for a high-quality racing bike if they won't actually buy it.

A financial statement showing a business's profit or loss, like the simple one shown here, can help you understand the importance of setting a fair sales price so that your business can earn a real profit. The total sales, or **gross value,** is the whole amount of money taken in before any costs are subtracted. The **net profit** is the money remaining after all costs for operating the business have been subtracted from the gross. That net profit is the *actual* money made by the business. Although all business owners hope their businesses will always return a net profit, there are times when those businesses may operate at a loss. Consider what would happen if your selling price for cookies was set too low and your sales in October came to only $200, while your operating costs were $207.50. In that case the business would have a **net loss** of $7.50. Although a net loss is not a good thing, it is necessary that you find out why it happened and what has to change so that it will not happen again. Profit and loss statements need to be prepared each month.

Profit and Loss Statement
Uncle Mark's Delicious Chocolate Chip Cookies
July 2009

Profit and Loss Statement
Uncle Mark's Delicious Chocolate Chip Cookies
August 2009

Profit and Loss Statement
Uncle Mark's Delicious Chocolate Chip Cookies
September 2009

Profit and Loss Statement
Uncle Mark's Delicious Chocolate Chip Cookies
October 2009

Total sales:		$350.00
Costs:		
Ingredients:	$170.00	
Paper to wrap cookies:	$ 25.00	
Electricity:	$ 1.75	
Advertising:	$ 10.75	
Total operating costs:	$207.50	−$207.50
Net profit:		$142.50

Chapter 7

Preparing Your Business Plan

Now it's time to focus on preparing your business plan. It might look something like this:

A Sample Business Plan

<u>Business name</u>: Debbie's Math Tutoring Service

<u>Service to be provided</u>: Tutoring service in all math topics taught at elementary school levels, to be given in time periods of 30 minutes before or after school, or on weekends and holidays.

<u>Customers to be served</u>: Elementary students at Washington Elementary School who are having difficulty in math. According to published school reports, 25 percent of students are at risk of receiving an unsatisfactory grade. Therefore, a total of 100 of the 400 students in this school might need my service.

<u>Charge for service</u>: $10 for a 30-minute period. Suggested books used are to be bought by students from tutor. Recommended number of meetings: a minimum contract of ten meetings per student, one per week, for a total of $100.00.

<u>Estimate of number of tutoring periods per week and money earned</u>: During the school year, I can provide up to eight hours of tutoring services per week.

- Two 30-min. meetings each school day before or after school for four days = four hours
- Four 30-min. meetings each Saturday = two hours
- Four 30-min. meetings each Sunday = two hours

During the school year: Charge for each lesson is $10.00. If I teach 16 lessons a week, I would earn $160.00 a week.

During the summer: I estimate that I can provide up to six lessons a day, four days a week, for a total of 24 lessons per week. At $10 per lesson = $240.00 per week.

As the business grows, it may be possible to set up meetings for two or three students at the same time. In this event, each student will pay a fee of $7.50 for the 30-minute lesson. This will cost $15.00 per lesson for two students and $22.50 per lesson for three students.

<u>Operating costs</u>: A beginning cost for 20 math booklets @ $12.00 each = $240.00 This start-up cost will be repaid by selling the booklets to students being tutored. Other start-up costs: less than $10.00 for flyers advertising my service to be given to teachers and PTA members. There will be no costs for space rental or transportation, as tutoring lessons will be held in school or in my home.

<u>Funding source</u>: $250 from my bank account

<u>Possible starting date</u>: November of this year, after report cards are received

Making a checklist of the points you have covered is a good way to find out what stage you're at and what you still need to get done. It can also help you realize if you are heading in a wrong direction before you get too far along. As you review this checklist, be certain that you have given enough thought to each of these points. Answers that haven't been clearly thought through at this stage can come back to haunt you later.

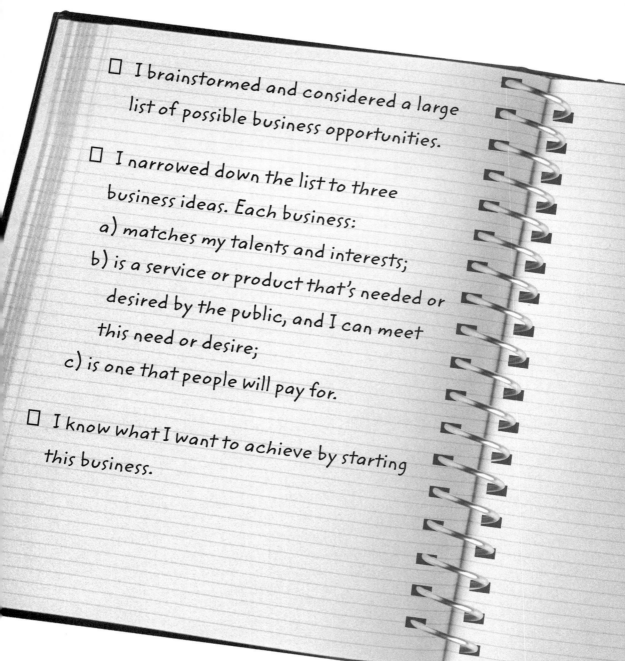

☐ I brainstormed and considered a large list of possible business opportunities.

☐ I narrowed down the list to three business ideas. Each business:
  a) matches my talents and interests;
  b) is a service or product that's needed or desired by the public, and I can meet this need or desire;
  c) is one that people will pay for.

☐ I know what I want to achieve by starting this business.

Review your business plan, making a checklist like the one below.

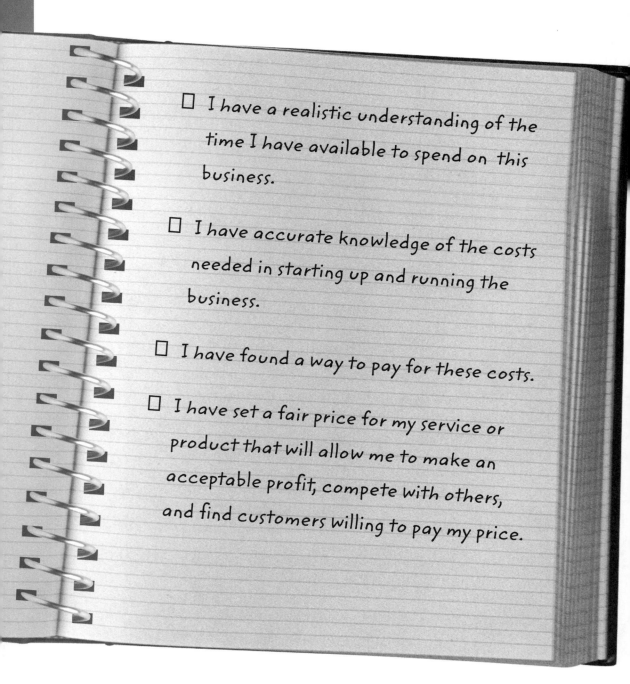

☐ I have a realistic understanding of the time I have available to spend on this business.

☐ I have accurate knowledge of the costs needed in starting up and running the business.

☐ I have found a way to pay for these costs.

☐ I have set a fair price for my service or product that will allow me to make an acceptable profit, compete with others, and find customers willing to pay my price.

Once you are sure that you've given enough thought to these issues, present your business plan to a few people who have experience starting and running a business. Ask whether they see any possible problems ahead or if there are any details you haven't addressed. While it is natural for you to want people to praise you and support your plans, it is more important that you make use of their special skills by asking them to point out any problems. A realistic evaluation of your plan can help you avoid major disasters along the way and be more successful later.

Pitfalls to Avoid

Listen carefully to the suggestions and advice of others. If someone feels that a part of your business plan won't work, pay attention! Make sure to look into any concerns they may have. Don't make the mistake of thinking that the problem will just go away as your business gets rolling. Fixing potential problems before they happen will prevent hassles.

You are almost ready to get started. Go over your plans in detail with your parents or anyone else who will be directly affected. Explain exactly what you are planning to do, why you are planning to do it, how much of your time and money you think it will take, and what, if any, help or support you'd like from them. Having people's support and encouragement will be a big help. And the opposite is true too—not having others on your side will cause you stress and could ruin your plans.

Once your business plan is done, the real work can begin! Are you eager and excited? Ralph Waldo Emerson, the famous philosopher, believed that nothing great could be done without enthusiasm. That certainly holds true for starting a business.

Chapter 8

Do You Need a Business Partner?

Now that you have prepared and reviewed your business plan, you may have found some problems, such as not having enough money or time to run the business, or that you're lacking a particular skill. One way to solve such problems is to consider taking on a business partner.

Selecting a partner should be done carefully because the long-term consequences of a bad choice can be serious. Naturally, you will want to choose someone you like because partners spend a great deal of time together. Liking someone isn't enough, however. In fact, many friendships have ended because of problems in a business partnership, so it might be best to pass over your closest friends when looking for a business partner.

Before you begin your business with a partner, it is very important that you both have agreed upon a plan. Clarify what each of your responsibilities will be, as well as how you will be paid and what percentage of the business each of you will own. This will prevent arguments later. In addition, it's a good idea to have a plan about what to do if you do not agree and cannot resolve the problem. Will one of you have final word? Will you go to a third person to make the decision?

The person you choose as a partner should be someone you respect and whose judgment you trust. Starting and growing a business requires making many choices and decisions. While it's unlikely that two people will agree on every point, you should be certain about your partner's intelligence and ability. Partners need to be able to rely on each other, whether or not they agree or disagree about specific business details.

Carefully consider the skills and interests you want a partner to bring to the business. Rather than looking for someone who is just like you, it would be more helpful if your partner has different abilities. For example, say you are really skilled at designing and creating but are not comfortable with the promoting and selling part of the business, then taking on a shy partner isn't a good idea. It would make much more sense for your partner to be a great communicator, a confident person who will be comfortable advertising your business. This would make it more likely that your business will succeed.

Or, if you are a natural **promoter** who loves to talk to people, but you can't stand sitting at a desk keeping **records**, then you need a partner who enjoys the record-keeping part of the business. Records must be kept accurately for your business to succeed, and if you don't want to do it, then make sure to find a partner who will.

Many successful businesses have been built upon the talents of a partnership team. Bill Gates and his partner Paul Allen started a software company called Microsoft and became billionaires. Calvin Klein, whose designer clothes are sold worldwide, started his business with a friend from school, and together they turned their dream into a worldwide success.

Make a contract that lists all that you have agreed to. This document should be signed by you and your partner. It should then be read and witnessed by someone who is not directly involved with the business. Each of you should keep a copy.

But not all business partners are successful. There can be quarrels and problems. Martha Stewart started out in the catering business with a friend, but as the business grew, so did the conflicts between them. As partners, they had different ambitions and conflicting ideas about how much time to devote to their business. The business partnership ended unpleasantly and so did their friendship.

The key is to make sure you and your partner have the same plans for your business, and that you come to an agreement about areas of responsibility and the time and energy each of you will be expected to give to the business.

Here's an example of how a contract may read:

A Partnership Contract

It is hereby agreed that [your name] and [partner's name] are equal partners in the start-up and operation of [name of business]. As equal owners we are equally responsible for all costs and will share equally in all profits. It is also agreed we will share equally in all work involved in providing services to our customers.

In the event that a disagreement should arise between us, it is agreed by both parties that [name of witness] will listen to both points of view and decide the action to be taken.

In the event that either of us wants or needs to end the partnership, one of the following actions will be followed:

- If we can agree on a fair value price for the business, the departing partner will receive half of that value in a full payment or in a payment plan to be completed within two years from the date of the agreement.
- If an agreement cannot be reached, the partnership will end and the company will cease to exist. If the company can be sold, then both partners will share equally in the money received. If the company cannot be sold, all equipment belonging to the company will be sold and funds split equally between the partners.
- In the event of a continued disagreement, it is agreed that [name of witness] will listen to both sides and decide how the partnership is to be ended and funds shared.

Signed_____   Date_____

Signed_____   Date_____

Witnessed by _____   Date_____

Pitfalls to Avoid

Your business partner must have good character and be willing to work hard.
Look for a partner who is honest, fair-minded, kind, intelligent, and responsible.
A business partner who lacks any of these characteristics will be a poor choice.

Chapter 9

Advertising to Find Customers

A brilliant idea, talent, funds, and hard work are essential for success in business, but you won't make any money if no one knows you have something to sell! The next step is to get out the word to potential customers, and that requires advertising. Giant businesses spend millions of dollars each year on advertising to attract customers. Their ads are everywhere: Internet, television, radio, billboards, magazines, and newspapers. They wouldn't spend so much money on those ads unless they were sure that the advertising brought in customers and helped them make money. Advertising is a good example of having to spend money to make money.

Like those successful companies, you will need to advertise, too. Since your business will be small, placing ads in popular media like television, radio, and newspapers will be far more expensive than you can afford. Fortunately, there are other less expensive ways to advertise. You can create a flyer explaining your services or products and your prices, as well as business hours. You might also give some information about yourself and your partner (if you have one). Photocopy the flyer for friends and family members. Be sure to show it to your parents before distributing it so they are aware of what you are doing. They might suggest some other ways to advertise your new business or be willing to hand out flyers to their friends. You can:

- Slip copies under your neighbors' doors.
- E-mail flyers to family and friends.
- Post the flyer or poster on the school bulletin board.
- Ask friends and family members to give flyers to their friends and family.

⚠ CAUTION!

Be careful about where you leave copies of your flyers or to whom you give them. If you are giving personal information on the flyers, make sure only friends and family members receive them. Talk to your parents about this—they'll have a good idea about what is safe.

Your flyer or poster should point out all the wonderful things about your product or service, and it needs to be clear. Here is a sample flyer for a business providing a grocery-shopping service for people who can't get to the store themselves.

Grocery Shopping Made Easy! One Call Does It All!

Finding it hard to make time to go grocery shopping?

Need help with the weekly shopping?

Forgot an item and need it now?

You can count on me!

I will get what is on your list.

I will get the brands you want.

I will deliver the groceries right to your door.

I am honest, responsible, and dependable.

Try me once, and you will use my services again and again!

$10.00 per store trip & delivery

Call Rhonda at the number listed below.

Bring in this flyer for one free shopping trip.

[One free shopping trip per customer, please.]

Here is another sample ad—this one for a tutoring service.

DO YOU HAVE MATH PROBLEMS?

Do you or someone you care about need help with addition, subtraction, multiplication, division, fractions, or percentages?

— Are these problems stressing you out? —
— Are they making you hate school? —
— Are they causing you to get poor grades? —

WELL, YOUR PROBLEMS ARE SOLVED!

Just one e-mail and all your math worries are over.
It's as simple as that.
E-mail me at CraigAPS@amazingmathwhiz.com
$10.00 per hour

WHO AM I?

I am an A student in math.
I am a great teacher and am very patient.
With me, you will not only learn math but also have fun while doing it.

Recommendations provided upon request.

Here is another sample ad, this time for a business that sells a product rather than one that provides a service.

Uncle Mark's Delicious Chocolate Chip Cookies
Never before available to the public!
No cookie tastes better!

Need a lift?
Thinking about the perfect dessert for your holiday dinner?
Wondering about just the right gift to give?

Try our super special chocolate chip cookies made from
a tried-and-true family recipe.
We are so convinced that you will love Uncle Mark's chocolate chip cookies
that we are making a special one-time only offer:
A free Uncle Mark's Chocolate Chip Cookie!

We know that one taste of an Uncle Mark's Chocolate Chip Cookie
will make you a fan for life.
For a short time only, we are offering Uncle Mark's Chocolate
Chip Cookies at a special introductory price:
6 cookies @ $4.50
12 cookies @ $8.00
24 cookies @ $15.00

Delivered fresh to your home the day they are baked!
All the information you need to contact me is listed below.

Chapter 10

Keeping Records

Operating a business requires many skills—one of the most important being the ability to keep good, up-to-date records. In the excitement of starting and growing a business, it is all too easy to forget the importance of keeping accurate records. You think: *I am too busy to write all of these things down now. I'll do it later when I have more time.* Procrastinating is a bad habit because it usually results in inaccurate records or no records at all!

The results of bad record keeping can be serious. You could miss appointments or delivery dates, fill orders incorrectly, or forget about money you owe for supplies. You might even think you are making more money than you actually are, which could result in spending money you don't have. You could anger customers or suppliers. You need to be aware at all times of how your business is doing—whether it's growing or failing. In order for your business to last and grow, you'll need to keep track of all costs in writing.

Costs

All of the costs for starting and operating the business need to be recorded. By knowing how much it costs to run your business every month, you can figure out how much money you'll need to make every month. This will also help you determine how many hours you'll have to work to make what you need.

It is important to record all **cash outlays** (no matter how small) immediately. After a day or two, it's easy to forget exactly how much you spent and for what. Make it a habit to keep all **receipts** from your purchases in an envelope and carry a notepad with you to list all items purchased, their exact cost, and the date of purchase. Be sure to record your daily **expenses**.

Cash Outlays Page
Uncle Mark's Delicious Chocolate Chip Cookies
December 2006

Cost* of ingredients:	$267.00
Cost of paper in which to wrap cookies:	$ 25.00
Cost for electricity (for oven and mixers):	$ 3.00
Cost of advertising:	$ 11.00
Total	$306.00

*Itemized costs of ingredients:

• Flour	$ 20.00
• Sugar	$ 9.00
• Brown sugar	$ 14.00
• Baking soda	$ 1.00
• Butter	$ 60.00
• Chocolate chips	$140.00
• Eggs	$ 14.00
• Vanilla	$ 8.00
• Salt	$ 1.00

Order Forms

Write down the key points that you and your customer have agreed on, then both of you sign the **order form**. Include the following on the order form:

- the specific item or service ordered;
- the amount the customer will pay you for the item or service;
- the date when you plan to deliver the item or service to the customer.

In addition, set a **cancellation policy** to protect yourself. What if you missed a fun day at the lake with friends because you agreed to mow someone's lawn for ten dollars. Then when you got there, the person didn't want the lawn mowed after all! It's too late to join your friends at the lake, *and* you are out the money, as well as any expenses (bus fare, for example). This isn't fair to you. Protect yourself by noting on the order form (previously signed by you and the customer) that customers will be charged if they don't cancel 24 hours in advance.

Order Form

I, _____ [Homeowner] hereby agree that _____ [Name of Individual] will mow my lawn the second and fourth Tuesday of every month.

I will pay _____ [Name of Individual] $10 each time my lawn is mowed.

In case of rain or other problem requiring cancellation, service will be provided by Lawn Mower to Homeowner on the following day.

If I, _____ [Homeowner], need to cancel for any reason, I must give _____ [Name of Individual] 24 hours notice, or I will be responsible for the entire $10 cost for lawn mowing.

Signed,

_____
[Homeowner]

_____
[Name of Individual]

Transactions

Keep a written record of all the orders you've received. This list of **transactions** should have a column for each of the following: the item or service, the cost, the amount the customer has paid so far, and the amount the customer still owes. Make sure to date each transaction.

Transactions

Date	Item/Service	Cost	Customer Paid	Customer Owes

Calendar

Keep a neat and organized calendar listing all of your promised products or services. This should include the date, time, and address for deliveries of ordered products and/or promised services. Include everything needed to do these services as well. Promptly write this information on your calendar so you don't forget any details. Also, keep a log of completed orders, recording the date that the task was finished.

June 2009 Calendar for Deliveries

Sun	Mon	Tues	Wed	Thurs	Fri	Sat
					1	2
3	4 12:00 2 doz. cookies to Garcia 10 Pine Street	5	6	7 4:00 3 doz. cookies to Grant 20 Elm Street	8	9
10 5:00 1 doz. cookies to Bates 8 Hilltop Drive	11	12	13	14 10:00 2 doz. cookies to Cohen 15 Oak Lane	15	16
17	18 10:00 1 doz. cookies to Kelly 51 Tulip Lane	19	20	21	22 5:00 3 doz. cookies to Spano 32 Oak Drive	23
24	25	26	27 12:00 1 doz. cookies to Bailey Ivy Terr. #B	28	29	30

Sales Charts

To keep track of how your business is doing, write down all of your sales and earnings on a weekly, monthly, and seasonal basis. Knowing how much money you are likely to make in the following weeks or months can help you budget your funds and your time. It will also help you see whether there are certain times when you are busier and other times when business drops off. For example, your sales charts might show that your tutoring service is busier and makes more money right before your local school gives tests. Knowing this will help you clear your schedule at those times so that you can take on more jobs and make more money.

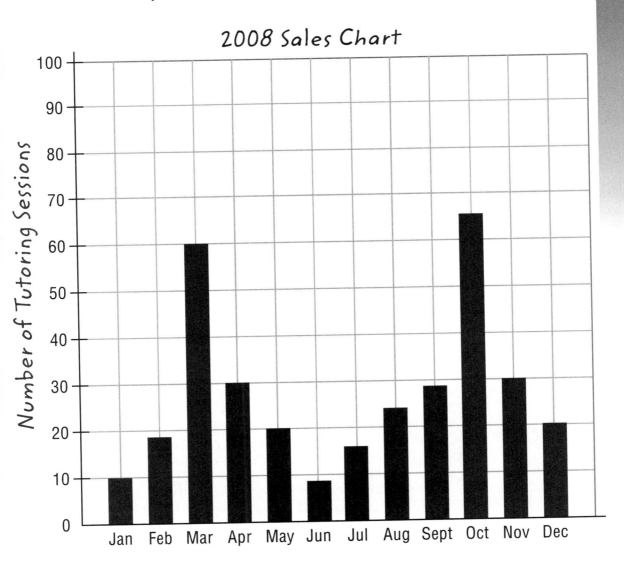

2008 Sales Chart

Chapter 11

Growing Your Business

By now you've learned that starting a business takes time, energy, and talent. You will face many challenges getting your business started, but if you work hard and stick with it through the hard times, then you can be a success. Once that happens, your next challenge is to expand your business. Your business may be doing just fine, but without growth or change, things can become dull. You might want to try something different, such as livening up your product or service so that your customers remain interested. Or you may want to make more money. These are all reasons why growth in a business is important.

Once you have answered the following questions, you'll be able to work on a new business plan.

- How do I get new customers while keeping the customers I have?
- Will I need to offer more products or services? If so, what could they be?
- What added costs will I have?
- Will I need to hire **employees**? If so, how will I train and pay them?
- Do I need to change the prices I charge?

How to Get New Customers

If the customers you already have are happy with the service or product you provide, they will be glad to recommend you to their friends and relatives. Customers can be a great form of advertising, so don't be shy about asking them to tell others about you, or asking if you can use their names as examples of satisfied customers. You can even ask if you can call some of their friends directly.

You might get customers to tell others about you by offering them an incentive. For example, for each new customer they bring in, you could deduct $5 from their next bill. You'd be surprised at how saving money can get people talking!

New Services or Products to Offer

Think carefully about the services or products you are now offering. What would be natural to add to what you are already doing? For example, if you are already offering lawn mowing, edging, and grass pickup, consider adding shrub clipping, weeding, and planting to the list of services you offer. Think about it—you already have the customer and the scheduled time to be at his or her home, so why not offer additional services for which you can earn more money?

Think the same way about a product you are selling. For example, if you have loyal customers for your chocolate chip cookies, think about adding other baked goods, such as low-fat items, to your line of products. Not only will some of your regular customers buy the new items, but you'll get new customers who might not be cookie lovers but will enjoy the new baked items you are offering. Explore your options!

Additional Costs

By adding to the services or products you offer, your costs will most likely increase. Figure out how much your costs will increase, then decide whether the money you will make on sales justifies the added costs. Will you be able to pass on those costs to your customers by raising your price? If so, how much more can you charge? Any additional products or services you offer should increase your profits in the long run, though for a short period of time, the added costs might result in less profit. If added sales haven't increased your profits after a few months, you need to reconsider your new business plan.

Make sure your customers realize that you're charging more because you're offering more. If they don't understand this, they may focus on the extra costs without considering the additional products and services. Explain to your customers that the changes will help them. This way, they won't question whether or not to continue doing business with you.

Pitfalls to Avoid

Don't take on more than you can handle. You won't gain anything if the cost of getting a new customer means losing one. And you will lose customers if you can't fill orders on time or if you provide less service than you used to because of having to rush off to another job.

Hiring Employees

You might decide to hire employees or take on another partner to help you handle the increased business. Think carefully about this decision. A good employee will help build your business, but a bad one may create problems. Your customers will view your employee as a part of your business. If your employee is rude or unreliable, that is the way your customers will look at you and your business. This could lead to lost **revenue**.

Make sure that your new employees are the kind of people you would want to represent you. They must be polite to customers and honor their commitments. Carefully train employees about their responsibilities, including the importance of acting professionally. Above all, make certain that your employees take pride in their work and care about the success of your business. Many employers offer bonuses, such as extra vacation or money, to employees who work extra hard, which usually makes them want to do their best.

Tip ➡ If you start your own business, you must have a social security number. Your business partner or any employees you hire will have to have one as well.

EMPLOYEE INTERVIEWS TODAY

Chapter 12

Keeping Customers Happy

Do you know what all successful businesses have in common? Satisfied customers. Making customers happy is the best way to keep their business, which means a steady source of **income** for you.

Many successful businesses develop questionnaires for their customers to find out whether their customers are satisfied. You often see these **surveys** in restaurants and hotels. Customer satisfaction surveys are a great way to find out what you are doing well and what you need to improve. By keeping customer surveys anonymous—that is, not asking for names on them—you are more likely to get honest feedback. Such information is extremely valuable. Here is an example of a customer satisfaction survey:

JOEY'S LAWN CARE SERVICE

Your business is very important to me. That's why I hope you will take a few minutes to complete this survey and let me know how I am doing. I promise to take your answers seriously and use them to help me improve my service to you.

Please circle a number 1 through 5 with 1 *terrible*, **2** *poor*, **3** *okay*, **4** *good*, **and 5** *excellent*.

1. I like the way my lawn is mowed.   1 2 3 4 5

2. I like the way my lawn is edged.   1 2 3 4 5

3. I like the way grass clippings are removed.   1 2 3 4 5

4. My lawn is mowed in a timely manner.   1 2 3 4 5

5. I find Joey to be polite and friendly.   1 2 3 4 5

Any other thoughts to help me serve you better are appreciated:

_____

_____

_____

_____

_____

_____

Read the completed surveys carefully. Knowing what your customers like about your product or service is important because you can put their quotes on new flyers advertising your business. More important, however, are the areas that your customers feel need improving. Take all comments seriously, using them to come up with ideas about how to improve your work. Remember that the customer who complains about a problem is more useful to you than the one who isn't satisfied, says nothing, and then stops doing business with you.

Think of other ways to acknowledge your loyal customers. Thanking them (in person or in writing) is a cost-free way to let customers know you value their business. Holiday cards are another way to show that you appreciate your customers.

Remember, though, that keeping customers depends on how good your product or service is. If you provide excellent products or services, you will have satisfied customers.

Everyone makes mistakes, however, and sometimes things go wrong. For example, you might get an order wrong or forget about an appointment. When that happens, admit you made an error. If you don't admit your mistake, you will upset your customers. You'd be surprised at how often an immediate and sincere apology can smooth things over.

But remember that not every customer who complains is right. When a customer is wrong, your response may determine whether you keep or lose that customer. There's an old saying in business: "The customer is always right"— even when he or she isn't. Although you want to keep your customers satisfied, don't admit to anything you didn't actually do. When customers complain, however, don't get angry or upset either.

CAUTION!

Sometimes you have a customer who always complains and is unfair in his or her dealings with you. Customers like this will hurt your business in the long run. Your best move is to end the business relationship quickly and carefully. Be sure to end your association politely, however. An angry ex-customer can spread damaging rumors about you and your business, so avoid the temptation to rebuke the person!

CUSTOMER
APPRECIATION
DAY

FREE
Cheesecake
with Every
Purchase!

Thank You

Chapter 13

A Time to Reflect and Adjust

Once you've got your business started, take some time to think about all you've been able to do. You started your own business—that's quite an accomplishment! You watched it grow from an idea to a real-life business, which earns you money and satisfaction.

Congratulate yourself. Then think about what you had hoped to achieve when you first began this business and what you actually accomplished.

You will probably realize that not everything went the way you thought it would. Perhaps some things exceeded your expectations while others were disappointing or turned out differently. Problems are to be expected. What's important is that you recognize how you were able to accomplish what you did. It's also important to figure out what went wrong and understand the reason it didn't work out so that you can do it differently in the future.

What do you want from your business in the future? Are your goals and expectations the same as when you began, or have they changed? Change is a part of life. As you gain experience, you may notice your needs and goals changing. That's why it is important to stop and reflect on your business. What do you need to do? And how will you make that happen?

If you want your business to do well, you must always be aware of the changing needs and desires of your customers, of new competitors, and of increasing costs. This means you constantly have to look around for new and better services and products that you can offer to your customers.

 Tip If profits grow large enough, taxes may need to be paid. Talk to an **accountant** or knowledgeable adult about keeping financial records and paying taxes.

You cannot depend on your past successes and believe that things will continue to go well without additional effort. To maintain a successful business, you must constantly think about and adjust it. Read the paper and search the Internet for the latest business ideas. The best companies change with the times and stay ahead of their competitors. They do not allow newcomers to outdo them. Always keep your eyes open for new competitors and other ways to improve your business. You never know where a great idea will come from!

Creating and growing your own business can give you a sense of pride. It will make you more confident, more aware of the needs and wants of others, . . . and hopefully richer! Good luck, and have fun!

 You can get free advice to help you start up and run your business from SCORE, a not for profit group and partner of the U.S. Small Business Administration. The website is www.score.org and the toll free phone number is 1-800-634-0245.

Bonus Chapter!

Starting a Publishing Company: A Group Project

There are times when a class or social group needs to raise money. Perhaps your teacher has suggested an exciting end-of-the-year class trip, but the only way it will happen is if the class can raise enough money to pay for the bus trip. Or maybe a club you belong to wants to have a party or donate money to a charity. You need to find a way to pay for those things.

Parents will often set up fundraisers (craft fairs or bake sales, for example) to help classes raise money. An even better idea is for your group to raise the money by starting a business. A project like this will aid real-life learning and improve self-reliance. All the information and advice you learned from this book can be applied to a group working together just as easily as a person working alone.

There are many ways your group can raise money. You can become distributors of products such as candy, calendars, and magazines, or you can create and sell craft items such as jewelry, potholders, and baskets. Those ideas are fine but aren't very unusual.

Instead, consider the talents and interests of the group when choosing which business to start. One idea is to start a publishing business. Surely some of the kids in your school are good writers. The group probably has a few talented artists too. Would those kids like to see their work published? Ask around…the answer to these questions will surely be a great big YES! Their skills and eagerness lend themselves well to starting a publishing business.

Let's take a closer look at this publishing business idea to see if it really will work. What would you publish? It has to be something that your group is able to complete within a certain time period. Some ideas are joke and riddle books, cookbooks, and books of poems, short stories, or essays. Everyone in your class can help with books like these. If you spread out the work, then it will get done more quickly. You also might think about publishing non-book items, such as calendars, bookmarks, and greeting cards.

At this point you have the idea, skills, interest, and time needed to start this publishing business. The next question is: How much will it cost to print your product? Figure out these costs by getting a price list from a local printer or copy shop. Make sure you can afford these costs or can get loans from families, town organizations, or perhaps even the school PTA. You also need to ask: Who will buy the materials that your class publishes? Who are your customers likely to be? It will partly depend on the type of books you publish. Adults are more likely to purchase cookbooks or calendars, kids will probably go for joke books and short stories, and everyone uses bookmarks. But it's important at this stage to know who your customers might be. You can do this in a brainstorming session with your group.

Possible Customers:

- Students and teachers in your school
- Parents and other relatives of the kids whose writing is published
- Neighbors and friends
- The local library

This list is just to get you started. You will probably think of other potential customers near your home. Once you've figured out the people you need to reach, you'll want to ask them what type of materials they would most likely buy. Ask a few kids from the group to be on the survey committee. They will be responsible for developing the simple survey, then listing the results and sharing them with the rest of the group. Everyone in the group will help hand out copies of the survey to potential customers and collect the completed surveys.

Each person in the group should ask at least five people to fill out the survey. If you have ten people in your group, that gives you at least 50 completed forms to use as your market survey, depending on the size of your group. The survey committee can list the results and share them with the rest of the group. The survey results will serve as your guide as to what to publish. But don't just go with the number one choice. Publish the top two or three choices. Your product will appeal to more people, and you will have more customers.

Survey

Our class is starting a publishing business to raise funds for a class trip at the end of this school year. In order to serve you better, we'd like to find out the type of materials that you would be most likely to buy. Please take a moment to rate this list of items from 1 to 5, with 1 being something that you are likely to purchase, 2 being something you probably will purchase, 3 being something you're not sure you'd purchase, 4 being something you probably won't purchase, and 5 being something that you definitely would not purchase. Thank you for your time and interest. We look forward to doing business with you.

4 **Our Classroom Cookbook: Favorite Family Recipes**

3 **Quick and Simple Recipes to Make Our Mouths Water**

4 **Healthy Foods Kids Love**

3 **Jokes for All Occasions**

5 **Riddles That Make You Think**

2 **Poems That Make You Laugh**

2 **Science Fiction Tales**

5 **Mystery Tales**

3 **Our Classroom Calendar**

3 **Greeting Cards for All Occasions**

The next point your group needs to address is **finances**. Once you know what you are going to publish, think about how you will get the materials necessary. The great thing about a publishing business is that you already have the brain power (special writing and art talent, good jokes) and most of the equipment (colored pencils, markers, scissors, rulers, computers) you'll need in your homes or classrooms.

Now that you've worked out the start-up costs and have a clear direction as to the type of materials you are going to publish, it's time for your group to begin writing. Set a **deadline** and arrange for all the writers to meet several times before the deadline. These meetings will make sure that no one leaves the writing until the last minute. Writers can brainstorm to help others get over their writer's block. Sometimes it's hard to get started, but if everyone works together to share ideas, it might help get the creative juices flowing. Later you may want to set up artists' meetings to serve the same purpose.

Even if the writers decide not to meet during the writing process, they need to understand that they must meet their deadlines. Set specific due dates for all stories, recipes, and jokes based on when you need to start selling the final product. Decide whether to limit written materials to those in your group or whether to ask for submissions from other kids in your school. If you decide to accept writings from other schools, you'll have to decide how to **broadcast** what type of writing you want and how long the pieces should be.

As the materials start coming in, you'll need to form committees to finish all the tasks needed to publish your book or books. It's a good idea for everyone to get involved and join at least one committee. This way, the whole group will take ownership of the project and will get the experience of starting a business. There will be plenty of work, and people with different skills and interests will be needed. There is sure to be something of interest to everyone. Here are some committees to consider forming, as well as their responsibilities.

Publishing Committee

This group explores questions such as the size and number of pages of the publication. For example, should it be 24, 48, or 64 pages long? Will it be in color or black and white? If you are planning to create greeting cards, will they be sold individually or in sets of 5, 10, or 15? How many different card designs should you create? Will the cards cover various occasions and holidays or will they just focus on birthdays? Once the publishing committee has decided what they think would be the most appealing to customers, they then present the choices to the finance committee.

Finance Committee

The finance committee gives advice to the publishing committee. It considers each of the suggestions made by the publishing committee and finds out how much each option will cost. This committee must always keep in mind that the goal is to raise money and keep costs down. The finance committee then works with the publishing committee to decide on the final product.

The finance committee will compare the costs of various printing options: whether to work with a print shop, for example, or to print the products using desktop publishing software on a school or home computer. They will work out whether to print in full color or black and white.

In short, the finance committee is responsible for the **bottom line**— the money, or profit, you will have after all of the costs to create and print the materials have been paid. This committee has to pay careful attention to expenses. Controlling costs is a major responsibility of the finance committee, and they make all such decisions.

Selection Committee

This group reviews all of the materials that are turned in. The selection committee will read and rate all entries for quality. It's a good idea for this group to meet before reviewing the materials to make sure everyone agrees on how to judge them.

Before the materials go to the selection committee, an impartial person should assign a number to all entries to replace the authors' names and record which number goes with which name. This way, selection committee members won't know who wrote each piece and won't be able to judge entries based on personal opinions. For example, a reader might want to give special favor to a good friend or might not be fair about the writing of someone he or she doesn't like. Removing the names will keep the judging fair. Entries should be accepted only on the basis of quality and suitability for publication. Once the materials have been chosen, artists can begin working on their selected pieces.

Editing Committee

The editing committee works with the chosen authors and artists to prepare the materials for publication. They will correct grammatical or spelling mistakes, and they might think of a more exciting ending to a story or suggest ways to change a particular drawing. Overall, they are making sure the final product is excellent—in content and style. After all, your paying customers deserve to get quality work.

Layout and Design Committee

The Layout and Design Committee works with the artists and the editing committee to put the writing and illustrations into an attractive design for publication. This group will decide what materials should go on each page and make sure the pages are readable and appealing. They will also come up with a design for the cover. They may be responsible for pasting up each page, which will then be brought to a copy shop to be photocopied and then pasted or stapled together. Or they might use desktop publishing software to design the publication on the computer, and then put together and prepare the pages themselves.

Advertising and Sales Committee

The advertising and sales committee sets a sales goal and develops a sales plan to achieve it. For example, if the amount your class needs to raise is $500, then that becomes the sales goal. This committee needs to figure out how many copies of your publication have to be sold to meet that goal. They will work closely with the finance committee to figure out costs for the product. For example, if creating the publication will end up costing the class a total of $200, then the amount of money needed to be raised is $700 ($200 pays for the costs and then $500 is left over to pay for the class event).

Keeping these figures in mind, the advertising and sales committee (working with the finance committee) must set the price of each publication. They need to figure out, for example, if the product can successfully be sold at $5.00. Will customers pay that price? Can the price be even higher?

They will need to make calculations such as: 140 copies will need to be sold at a price of $5.00 each to make the sales goal (140 x $5.00 = $700, which covers $200 for costs, leaving $500 net profit for the class event). Then they need to figure out if it's possible to sell 140 copies. They will do this by coming up with creative ways to sell the product, including advertising. It would be smart to speak with an adult who works in sales for some tips.

Timeline

Once committees have been set up and class members know their responsibilities, it's time to figure out a **timeline**. For example, if your class trip will be at the end of June but you need to pay for it a few weeks ahead of time, then you will need to have the money in hand by June 1. By working backward from your "money due" date, you can decide what steps need to happen when.

Everyone involved must understand that each due date must be met. Once one date is missed, then the whole schedule can fall behind. This could result in your group not making the money it needs. To keep from missing dates, allow plenty of extra time in the schedule for those unexpected problems that always seem to happen. Here is a sample schedule. Fill in your own dates.

Schedule	
Final date for receiving written materials and art	January 1
Final decision from selection committee as to which pieces will be included in publication (*allow two weeks*)	January 15
Final date for receiving artwork (artwork should decorate or explain written pieces) (*allow three weeks after selection of written pieces*)	February 8
Complete, error-free text due from editing committee (*allow at least three weeks after selection of written pieces*)	February 10
Completely designed cover and materials due from design and layout committee and are ready for printing (*allow four weeks*)	March 10
Printed books/product due (*allow three weeks*)	March 31
Month-long sales effort begins	April 1
End of sales period (*a few weeks before final money for class trip is due so any money owed can be collected on time*)	May 1
FINAL GOAL: Funds needed for trip ($500)	June 1

It's the publishing committee's responsibility to keep track of the schedule and make sure that the due dates are met. Without doubt, problems will occur, but if the schedule is carefully tracked, other plans can be set in motion and the final deadlines met.

When the sales and marketing period begins, then the finance committee needs to go over all bills and pay them on time. They also need to collect all the money and keep accurate records of everything received and spent. They should place the money in a bank account, making sure to record each piece of business.

The planning and effort that your group puts into your classroom business will most likely result in meeting your goal of raising money. In addition, your group will learn valuable business skills and find out how a business works from the inside. You will feel great pride for a job well done!

This book was written to help you develop the ability and confidence to be successful in business. The skills and strategies you learned from reading this book can help you start your own business and earn some extra money now, and they will also continue to be useful throughout your life. One of the most important things to remember is that you don't need to sit back and wait for someone else to give you money or a job or the things you want and need in your life. You can and should go after what it is you want or need yourself. Opportunity is everywhere.

There's an old saying that carries an important truth: "Give a person a fish and that person has food for one day. Teach a person to fish, and that person has food for a lifetime." This book offers knowledge and information that will help you "learn to fish"—that is, to be more independent and self-sufficient. Wishing you much success in your new business!

accountant	a professional who helps individuals with business concerns, including the inspection and preparation of financial records
advertisement	speech, written pieces, pictures, or film used to convince people to buy something
bottom line	the profit or loss shown after all costs to a business have been figured out
broadcast	to make widely known
business plan	a written plan that lists the past, present, and future of the company, usually used to apply for a loan. It tells what is to be done and how to do it.
cancellation policy	a course of action decided upon when customers change their minds about something they originally wanted
cash outlays	money one spends for a business
competitor	someone who competes (tries for something wanted by others, such as a prize or reward), often in the selling of goods and services
consulting	to work as one who gives expert or professional advice.
contract	the terms and conditions of an agreement shown in writing
credit rating	a statement of the amount of credit, or money, that can be given, based on a person's or business's ability to pay back that loan in a timely manner
deadline	a date or time by which something must be completed
discount	an amount subtracted from a regular price
distributor	someone who markets or sells products
employee	a person who works for someone else
expenses	money spent, for example, to run a business
finances	money available to a business or individual
gross value	the whole (for example, amount of money) before necessary deductions have been made

guarantee	a promise that something will work or happen the way it should
income	money coming in from business, work, or other endeavors
innovations	new ideas, methods, or things
interest	the money paid by a borrower in order to use borrowed money
investing	spending time, energy, and/or money for later good or profit
loan	the permission to use something (often money) with the understanding that it will be paid back at a later date
loan officer	a person, usually at a bank, who helps business owners get a loan
manufacturer	one who makes products from raw materials by hand or machine
net loss	loss remaining after all charges and expenses have been subtracted
net profit	profit remaining after all charges and expenses have been subtracted
ongoing costs	costs that continue
order form	a form to use when placing an order
product	something produced by manufacture or labor
profit	the gain after all expenses have been subtracted from the total amount received
promoter	one who works hard at forming a business or helping it grow
questionnaire	a list of questions to be asked of a number of people to gather facts about their opinions or knowledge
receipts	written statements indicating that something has been received or paid for
records	facts written down to keep information available
revenue	money taken in
service	work done for others as a business
start-up costs	the costs to start a new business or operation
survey	a gathering of a sample of data or opinions to learn facts about a business
timeline	a schedule of deadlines or events
transaction	a business deal